MOVIE VOCAL SELECTIONS

CHICAGO

12	AND ALL THAT JAZZ
20	FUNNY HONEY
24	WHEN YOU'RE GOOD TO MAMA
29	CELL BLOCK TANGO
44	ALL I CARE ABOUT
49	WE BOTH REACHED FOR THE GUN
61	ROXIE
64	I CAN'T DO IT ALONE
71	MISTER CELLOPHANE
76	RAZZLE DAZZLE
82	CLASS*
87	NOWADAYS
90	I MOVE ON

*Not in the film, but included on the soundtrack.

MIRAMAX FILMS PRESENTS A PRODUCER CIRCLE CO. PRODUCTION

A ZADAN/MERON PRODUCTION

RENÉE ZELLWEGER   CATHERINE ZETA-JONES   AND RICHARD GERE   "CHICAGO"

QUEEN LATIFAH   JOHN C. REILLY   LUCY LIU   TAYE DIGGS   COLM FEORE   CASTING BY LAURA ROSENTHAL & ALI FARRELL   COSTUME DESIGNER COLLEEN ATWOOD   MUSIC SUPERVISOR MAUREEN CROWE   EXECUTIVE MUSIC PRODUCERS RIC WAKE   RANDY SPENDLOVE   MUSIC SUPERVISED AND CONDUCTED BY PAUL BOGAEV

ORIGINAL SCORE MUSIC BY DANNY ELFMAN   CHOREOGRAPHED BY ROB MARSHALL   EDITED BY MARTIN WALSH   PRODUCTION DESIGNER JOHN MYHRE   DIRECTOR OF PHOTOGRAPHY DION BEEBE, ACS   CO-PRODUCER DON CARMODY   BASED ON THE MUSICAL PLAY "CHICAGO"   DIRECTED AND CHOREOGRAPHED FOR THE STAGE BY BOB FOSSE

BOOK OF THE MUSICAL PLAY BY BOB FOSSE & FRED EBB   MUSIC BY JOHN KANDER   LYRICS BY FRED EBB   PRODUCED ON THE STAGE BY ROBERT FRYER   JAMES CRESSON   MARTIN RICHARDS   IN ASSOCIATION WITH JOSEPH HARRIS   IRA BERNSTEIN   LYRICS AND MUSIC PUBLISHED BY UNICHAPPELL MUSIC INC.

BASED ON THE PLAY BY MAURINE DALLAS WATKINS   EXECUTIVE PRODUCERS CRAIG ZADAN   NEIL MERON   EXECUTIVE PRODUCERS HARVEY WEINSTEIN   MERYL POSTER   JULIE GOLDSTEIN   JENNIFER BERMAN   BOB WEINSTEIN   SAM CROTHERS

SCREENPLAY BY BILL CONDON   PRODUCED BY MARTIN RICHARDS   DIRECTED BY ROB MARSHALL

SOUNDTRACK AVAILABLE ON   SONY MUSIC SOUNDTRAX   DOLBY DIGITAL   dts   SDDS   READ THE NEWMARKET PRESS BOOK   www.miramax.com/chicago   MIRAMAX FILMS

ISBN 1-84328-380-8

IMP

International Music Publications Limited
Griffin House, 161 Hammersmith Road, London W6 8BS, England

FILM CAST AND CREW

Directed and Choreographed by Rob Marshall
Screenplay by Bill Condon
Produced by Martin Richards

Principal Cast:

Renée Zellweger..............ROXIE HART
Catherine Zeta-Jones .....VELMA KELLY
Richard Gere...................BILLY FLYNN
John C. Reilly ....AMOS HART
Queen Latifah ....MATRON "MAMA" MORTON
Christine Baranski............MARY SUNSHINE

SYNOPSIS
of the film adaptation

Everyone loves a legend, but in Chicago, there's only room for one. Velma Kelly (CATHERINE ZETA-JONES) burns in the spotlight as a nightclub sensation. When she shoots her philandering husband, she lands on Chicago's famed murderess row, retains Chicago's slickest lawyer, Billy Flynn (RICHARD GERE), and is the center of the town's most notorious murder case, only increasing her celebrity.

Roxie Hart (RENÉE ZELLWEGER), seduced by the city's promise of style and adventure, dreams of singing and dancing her way to stardom. When Roxie's abusive lover tries to walk out on her, she too ends up in prison. Billy recognizes a made-for-tabloids story, and postpones Velma's court date to take on Roxie's case. Infamy is Roxie's ticket to stardom. Billy turns her crime of passion into celebrity headlines, and in this town, where murder is a form of entertainment, she becomes a bona fide star—much to Velma's chagrin.

As Roxie fashions herself as America's sweetheart, Velma has more than a few surprises in store, and the two women stop at nothing to outdo each other in their obsessive pursuit of fame and celebrity. A new interpretation that takes the award-winning Broadway show into fresh and expansive cinematic realms, CHICAGO shifts adroitly from the reality of intrigue, rivalry and betrayal to spectacular fantasies of music and dance, offering tongue-in-cheek commentary on the cult of celebrity and the scandalous lengths to which people will go to attain it.

CHICAGO ON STAGE

CHICAGO – A Musical Vaudeville
Music by John Kander
Lyrics by Fred Ebb
Book by Fred Ebb and Bob Fosse
Based on the 1926 play *Chicago* by Maurine Dallas Watkins

The Original Broadway Production
Directed and Choreographed by Bob Fosse
Opened June 3, 1975 at the 46th Street Theatre

Principal Original Cast:

Gwen Verndon.............ROXIE HART
Chita Rivera ....VELMA KELLY
Jerry Orbach ....BILLY FLYNN
Barney Martin ....AMOS HART
Mary McCartney ....MATRON "MAMA" MORTON
M. O'Haughey ....MARY SUNSHINE

Of interest: during the run Liza Minnelli and Ann Reinking also played Roxie.

The Revival
Directed by Walter Bobbie
Choreographed by Anne Reinking (in the style of Bob Fosse)
Opened on Broadway on November 16, 1996 at the Shubert Theater

Principal New York Revival Original Cast:

Ann Reinking ....ROXIE HART
Bebe Neuwirth.............VELMA KELLY
James Naughton ....BILLY FLYNN
Joel Grey ....AMOS HART
Marcia Lewis ....MATRON "MAMA" MORTON
D. Sabella....................MARY SUNSHINE

The same production opened in London on November 18, 1997
at the Adelphi Theatre.

Principal London Original Cast:

Ruthie Henshall............ROXIE HART
Ute Lemper..................VELMA KELLY
Henry Goodman ....BILLY FLYNN
Nigel Planer................AMOS HART
Meg Johnson...............MATRON "MAMA" MORTON
C. Shirvell.....................MARY SUNSHINE

CHICAGO

AND ALL THAT JAZZ

Words by FRED EBB
Music by JOHN KANDER

Come on, babe,_ why don't we paint the town,_ And

all that jazz!_ I'm gon - na rouge my knees_ and roll my stock - ings down_

And all that jazz!_ Start the car,_ I know a whoop-ee spot_ where the

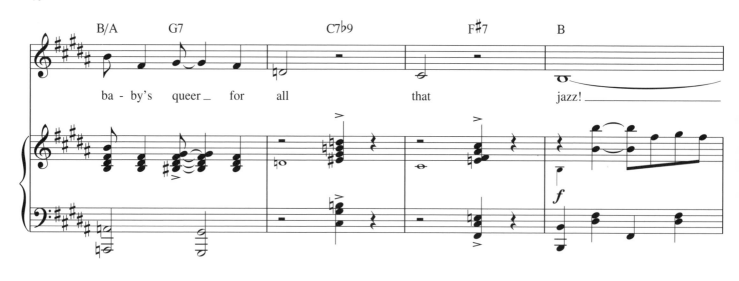

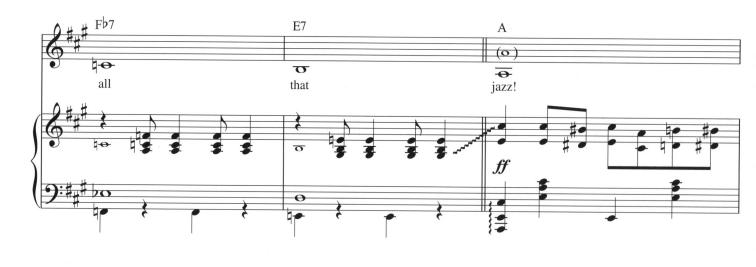

all that jazz!

FUNNY HONEY

Words by FRED EBB
Music by JOHN KANDER

* Sung an octave lower

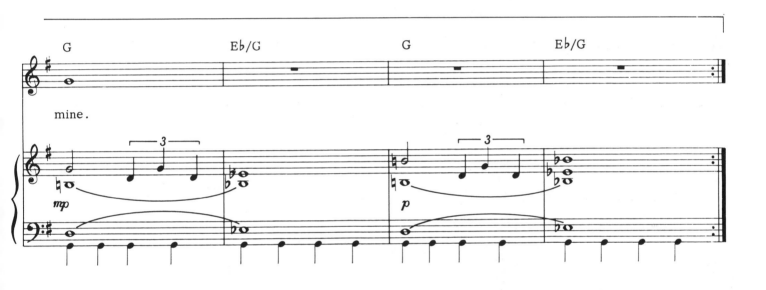

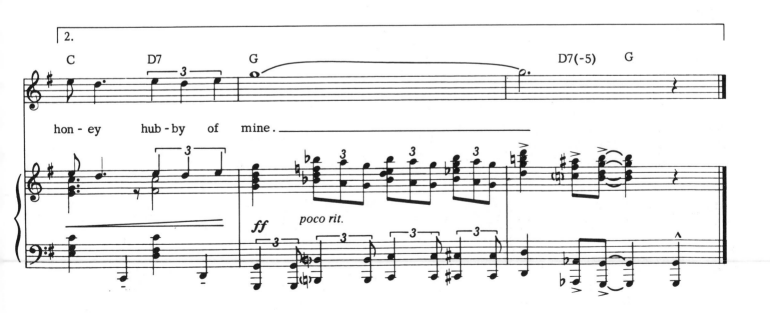

WHEN YOU'RE GOOD TO MAMA

Words by FRED EBB
Music by JOHN KANDER

Lyrics:
Ask an-y of the chick-ies in my pen. They'll tell you I'm the big-gest moth-er hen. I love them all and all of them love me Be-cause the sys-tem works, the sys-tem called re-ci-proc-i-ty!

* Sung an octave lower

28

CELL BLOCK TANGO

Words by FRED EBB
Music by JOHN KANDER

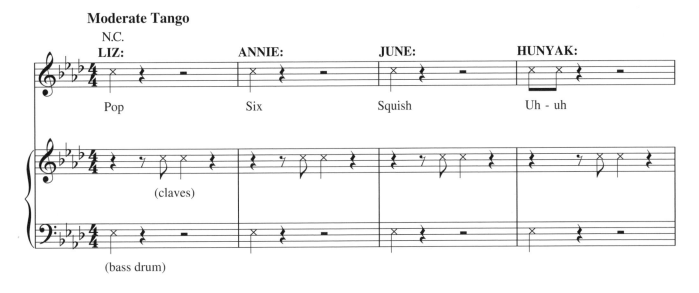

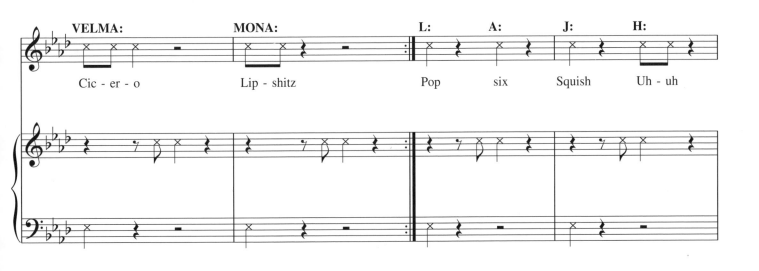

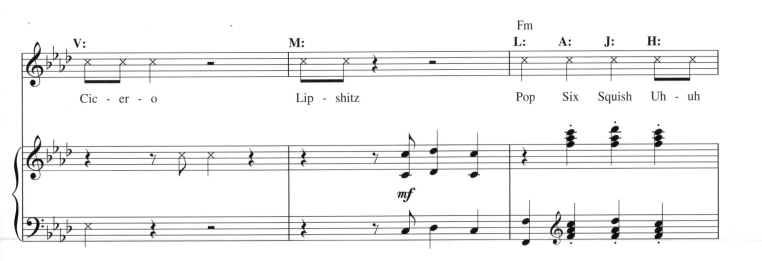

same. He had it com - in', he had it com - in', he on - ly

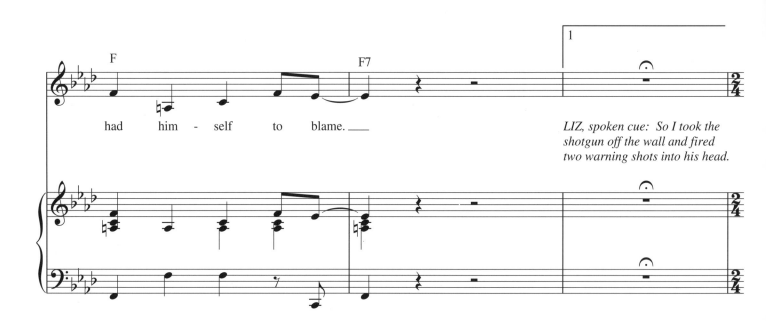

had him - self to blame. ____

LIZ, spoken cue: So I took the shotgun off the wall and fired two warning shots into his head.

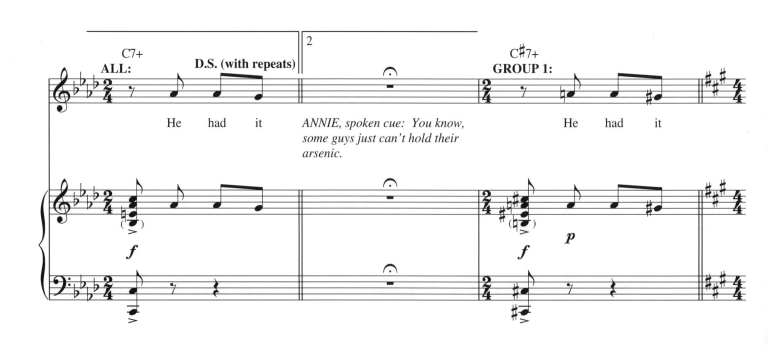

ALL: He had it

ANNIE, spoken cue: You know, some guys just can't hold their arsenic.

D.S. (with repeats)

GROUP 1: He had it

Bm   D7   C#7+   F#

(Hunyak speaks her story)

seen it,   I bet - cha   you   would   have   done   the   same.

B/F#   Bm/F#   D7/F#

F#m/C#   C#   F#

36

(2nd time: Stop at Velma's line: "Veronica and Charlie doin' number 17, The Spread Eagle.")

been there, if you'd have seen it,
used it, and he a - bused it.

I bet - cha you would have felt the same,
It was a mur - der, but not a crime.

He had it

Spoken (Velma continues): Well, I was in such a state of shock, I completely blacked out. I can't remember a thing! It wasn't until later, when I was washing the blood off my hands, I even knew they were dead!

VELMA:
They had it com - in', they had it com - in', they had it

ENSEMBLE:
They had it com - in', they had it com - in',

43

ALL I CARE ABOUT

Words by FRED EBB
Music by JOHN KANDER

46

WE BOTH REACHED FOR THE GUN

Words by FRED EBB
Music by JOHN KANDER

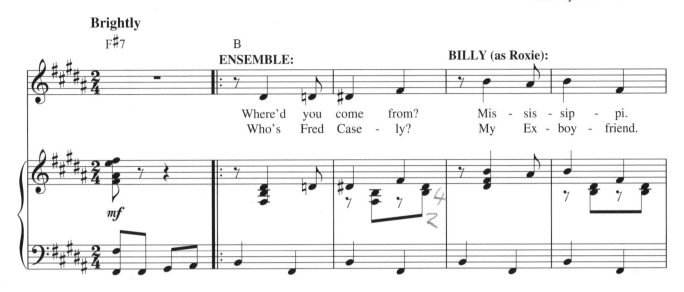

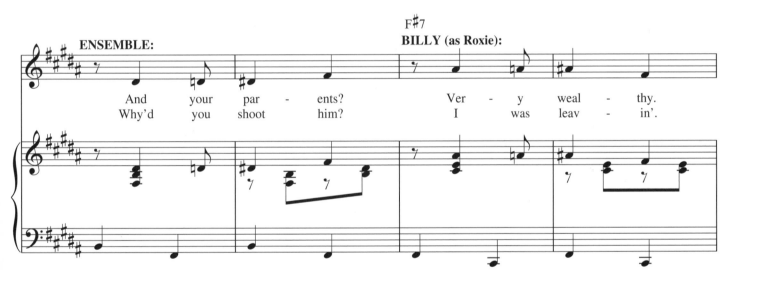

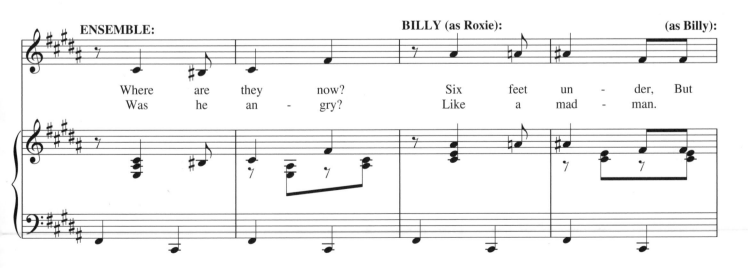

And he stole my heart a-way, con-vinced me to e-lope one day.

(as Billy): He had strength and she had none, And yet we both reached for the gun.

(Mary Sunshine speaks)

Oh yes, oh yes, oh yes,— we both, oh yes, we both, oh yes,— we both reached for

B13
yes, oh yes, they both, oh yes, they both, oh yes, they both reached for
E6
The gun, the gun, the gun, the gun, oh yes, they both reached for the gun,
BILLY: Now you got it!
accelerando
B7
E6
F
for the gun. Oh yes, oh yes, oh yes, they both,
C13
F
oh yes, they both, oh yes, they both reached for The gun, the gun, the gun,

ROXIE

Words by FRED EBB
Music by JOHN KANDER

I CAN'T DO IT ALONE

Words by FRED EBB
Music by JOHN KANDER

66

MISTER CELLOPHANE

Words by FRED EBB
Music by JOHN KANDER

RAZZLE DAZZLE

Words by FRED EBB
Music by JOHN KANDER

80

CLASS

Words by FRED EBB
Music by JOHN KANDER

NOWADAYS

Words by FRED EBB
Music by JOHN KANDER

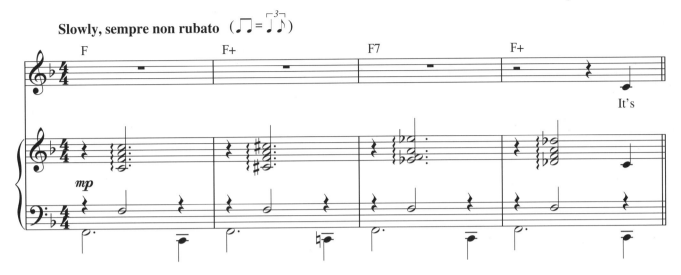

I MOVE ON

from the Motion Picture CHICAGO

Words by FRED EBB
Music by JOHN KANDER